FOREWORD

For many of us the medium of poetry offers us a voice - a voice to speak out and let others know what we feel, think and desire. It is the vital bridge of communication that lets us share our innermost thoughts and messages on life to people who may need that vital surge of poetic inspiration. It offers experience to those with none or little, spreads light to those in darkness and at the same time it encourages others that they are not alone.

Miracles Of Nature is a unique collection of poetry written in a variety of styles with the theme of the natural world around us. The poems are easy to relate to and encouraging to read, offering engaging entertainment to their reader.

This delightful collection is sure to win your heart, making it a companion for life and perhaps even earning that favourite little spot upon your bookshelf.

Editor
Clare Bull

MIRACLES OF NATURE

Edited by

Clare Bull

First published in Great Britain in 2002 by
ANCHOR BOOKS
Remus House,
Coltsfoot Drive,
Peterborough, PE2 9JX
Telephone (01733) 898102

HB ISBN 1 85930 177 0
SB ISBN 1 85930 182 7

CONTENTS

WINTER CAT

Soft and white
snowflakes fall,
you watch from the window
in the hall.

Stand amazed
at the scene,
everything is white now.
Where's the green?

Door ajar
out you go,
your very first pawprints
in the snow.

Paws outstretched
touch the ground,
playing with strange white stuff
that you've found.

Whiskers white,
winter cat
scurries back inside now,
finds the mat.

Snug and warm,
fire aglow,
dreams of her adventures
in the snow.

Angela Pritchard

THE CURIOUS CAT

He's very curious, wants to know
Who rolls the yellow ball
Across the sky by day and then,
When night comes, lets it fall.

He marvels that I stand erect
And have two legs not four.
His limbs can move as fast as mine.
Why does he need two more?

I've seen him nuzzling a peach,
Rummaging for its scent,
Looking for the intangible,
Wondering where it went.

What make-up artist, he reflects,
Puts rouge on apple cheeks,
Gives highlights to maturing pears
With subtle golden streaks.

He's mystified when spiders spin
Patterns of fragile lace,
Nosing through slender strands that twine
Around his puzzled face.

To him the moon's a fresh meringue -
It looks so crisp and light,
And all the sugar candy stars
Seem close enough to bite.

He thinks that butterflies absorb
Their colours from the rainbows.
He loves to watch their petalled wings
Shimmer where the sun flows.

He has a sense of wonderment,
Sleeps on a field of dreams,
Then wakes each day to beauties that
The rising sun redeems.

Celia G Thomas

CANINE HOLLY AND ME

Jack Russell Holly is nice to know,
Slender long legs down to each white paw;
We're both the same age in ratio,
She's ten in canine and I'm seven 'o';
She's as strong as an ox and doesn't look old,
I sometimes feel my age but look younger I'm told;
'Lead' is a word Holly knows how to spell,
She knows biscuits and tea-time and walkies as well;
She wags a warm welcome to callers we know,
Then barks madly at them when they get up to go;
Her aim is to please whatever she does,
Like sharing her toys with humans she loves;
She just comes to stay she isn't really mine,
But we're being twins this year, me, and Holly - canine.

Ivy Squires

JACKY AND LUKEY

Whatever the weather, wet or warm,
Icy cold or a summer storm,
Jacky and Lukey are ready to race
Through the fields at a galloping pace.

Jacky, in shining, feathery black,
White socks and shirt front, sprung steel back,
Is up through the fields with an eager cry
To chase the birds as they wheel and fly.

Lukey, with lissom, terrier grace,
Is close at his heels in the breakneck race.
Yelping and sniffing they quarter the land,
Perhaps there's a partridge close at hand.

Quick, there's a lark just skimming the ground
And her song is a taunting, challenging sound.
They're away as she soars through the pearly light
But she rises and climbs till she's lost to sight.

And the dogs come running with shining coats,
Their tongues hanging loose from their panting throats;
With a glint of a laugh in their dancing eyes
And a world of joy in their gasping sighs.

Flora Hughes

MY MOGGIE

What is it in a humble little cat
That purrs and spends long hours in sleep,
Then waking, makes a plea for that
Which does its furry texture keep?

Perhaps a tin of delicious meat
Or something dried in selection rare
To which the pinkish padded feet
Are drawn, for heights of ecstasy there.

What can it be that's in a pet so cute?
That scratches wood and wall and chair;
Though often a child substitute
A source of joy and yet despair.

Why is it that the owner can forgive
When playful nature causes harm?
Because it is so good to live
With one of such exquisite charm

Vere Collins

THE SURFER

Early morning walking on the beach
With blue skies so clear and bright
Then in the distance comes into sight
An excited and seemingly laughing dog
There with his master taking a stroll

A young eager big black Labrador, still a pup
Pulling his master nearer to the water's edge
Smile to myself morning stroll is that what I said
But this dog's heart is set on bouncing in the briny
His owner trying to keep him so well controlled
With his lead let out only a bit at a time
Just like a skilled fisherman with his reel

Then at last this lively dog takes to the ocean
So out into the sea he dashes and plunges
Into the oncoming waves he then splashes
There he goes under it, over it, then to return
Into the shore the bigger the waves the better
Then there he goes in again and again
Riding the waves like an expert surfer

Octavia Hornby

SET THEM FREE

Whenever Man sees an animal, he puts it in a cage
He thus incurs from heaven a rightful wrath and rage;
God didn't make these creatures to imprison behind bars,
He gave us open spaces and endless twinkling stars,
Yet Man locks up all beasts, and fellow humans too
'Tis thus he chains his heart and soul, forgets the truth he knew,
That all beings were made to live in joy, unfettered, glad and free
And not to serve as slaves or toys to a tyrant's cruel decree,
For even he who does dark deeds bears seeds of the divine,
And only love can save, restore, to let humanity shine.

Emmanuel Petrakis

WATER OUSEL

So
modest
in its ways,
nun-like and quick,
it curtseys and dips
baptismally. 'Sip.
Sip.' The laic
song displays
its breast:
snow.

Norman Bissett

A SWAN

A swan is such a splendid creature,
full of power and mystical elegance.
Which so bodes a special pleasure,
for us mere mortals to - on them glance.

An uplifting experience to view their splendour,
when they their wings - full spread.
And our hearts are openly rendered,
in admiration of them - is held.

The larger breed so full of white,
as rich as the powerful driven snow.
Then is spread - in total plight,
its enormous wings in ivory flow.

Treading water to achieve flight,
the heavy body - becoming heavenly.
In such a graceful marvellous sight,
to experience for me pleasantly.

And one magical thought I always have,
being those 'Wings of Love' divine.
As emotions we wish to grab,
but nature for us - does not incline.

Gary J Finlay

LITTLE EURO ONE

A Puzta dog with tribal inclinations
who rose to the new trend in international relations.
You came from the steppes of Hungary
finding your way into a German kennel.
A young lady in a foreign land,
was looking for a companion.
You were the choice and your name became *Morris*.
You clever little dog adjusted well
to commands given in German or English
but never losing your very own trait -
to be a faithful companion.

Augusta Cotterell

MY PAL

I wrote this rhyme, just for you.
Friend indeed, when I had few.
You came to me like a ray of sun.
Turned my darkest days to fun.

Ever ready for a game,
Or a long walk in the rain.
Your faith in me, and trust too.
Friendship that is real, and true.

Given without reward, or favour asked.
How many friends can that test pass?
Hope that we will always be,
The best of pals until eternity.

Because pals like you are very few,
And all seem to walk on four legs too.

G W Bailey

SYDNIA II, BLACK AND WHITE CAT

Sydnia II, black and white cat,
O, where light is singing
I am distraught and misled:
Reaction is not ambition,
It is undermining me:

The dove is alone,
It flies above, implicit,
Resolved to envision us,
Without selfish reason:

When clocks are burned,
To engage our deceit,
Emerge with one valour
Entreat our thoughts:

Edmund Saint George Mooney

CRAZY LADY

My little dog has grown quite fat,
Those tit-bits really have to stop.
Sometimes I think if her tail whizzed round,
She'd look like a torpedo!

She goes quite mad, when the postman comes,
And bounces round the floor.
And jumps and barks like crazy,
At the handle of the door.

I don't know why she gets het up,
To see what he has brought,
If she doesn't know there's none for her,
I think by now she ought.

She jumps onto my husband's knee
Her paws around his neck,
And with her sloppy long pink tongue
She gives his face a smack.

She makes such funny noises
When she thinks she's going walkies
If there was such an audition
She'd soon be on the 'talkies'.

A crazy lady she may be,
But she means such a lot to me.
I wouldn't be without her,
No siree!

Isobel Laffin

SOPHIE AND SMOKIE

*(In remembrance of Sophie and Smokie who had a few special years
of happiness with Barbara and Alan Baxter before passing onto
Rainbow Bridge)*

Sophie, dear Sophie, you didn't have a life, your bed was just
a wooden shed, you knew such pain and strife.
Till one day someone found you and carried you in her car.
She hope the vet could see you, it wasn't very far.
Your nails had grown into your pads, you crawled on elbows bare.
It broke my heart to see you cry. It really wasn't fair.
The tortured life in that dark shed, still haunts me to this day.
But now you have a nice warm bed, a garden where to play.
Your new mum has erased your past, and filled your heart with love.
You're kissed and loved and cherished and thought the whole world of.
Whilst lying in my bed one night I heard Mum say to Dad.
'We may as well adopt one more, a big blue handsome lad!'
So off we went to Aunty Pat's to bring our Smokie home.
He looked so sad and helpless, rejected and alone.
We soon became the best of friends and people would comment
How nice we were together. Happy and content.
But three years on I passed away and went to Rainbow Bridge.
Where I run and play with friends. In heaven o'er the ridge.
Far into the distant light I see a hound appear.
It looks like - God, oh yes it is.
It's Smokie and he's here. We walk together through the fields
Through pastures sweet and new. We'll never be apart again.
We've made it just us two.

Pat Bradley

CATS

Cats are canny
Cats are wise
Following life
With knowing eyes

They stand aloof
Independent souls
Deceiving humans
With feline roles

We kid ourselves
We own each puss
Not true at all
They own us!

L J Stuart

AN INCIDENT IN AN OPEN AIR ZOO

Grey adolescent look-alikes,
Each tethered to a barrel,
Sitting quietly in a line,
With no fear of man,
Under the Canadian sky.
Never have they roamed, forest free,
Like their wind forebears,
Afraid of man and by man feared.

A lady passes by; in spite of name above,
'No bars,' she thinks, 'no danger here.'
So she pets a canine head.
Like a dog he shows his pleasure;
But his neighbour, also stroked
Quietly goes into his barrel.
'Just like dogs' she thought,
'and unalike in nature as litter mates can be.'

'Wolves by nature killers?
No I have met dogs more fierce,
More dangerous, than these.'
Never more would I believe
Their evil reputation.
I love all the canine kind.

Frances Joan Tucker

MAX
(To Max, my little King Charles Spaniel)

As I follow the trail of dirty footprints,
On my newly cleaned floor,
I discover a furry figure,
Looking sheepishly at me from behind the door,
The sad eyed expression,
That imploring look,
'Please don't tell me off'
You can read him like a book,
The anger diminishes,
The annoyance subsides,
My facial expression softens,
Much to his delight,
With a wagging tail
And a sparkle in his eyes,
I'm sure he's only thinking
What next mischief he can devise,
But how can you resist
That cute little wet nose,
The bundle of fluff that always is in search of attention,
And to be cuddled and kissed,
Sometimes he gets under my feet,
Leaves his fur wherever he has been,
But he is still the soppiest, loveliest dog I've ever seen.

Michelle Luetchford

THE BIRD FEEDER

The squirrel runs sure-footed
Along the slippery branch.
Whither he goes who knows
Of his reasons for scurrying?
So, then stopping, then again
Hurrying to his hiding place
Amongst the thick ivy clad tree

One wet and windy morning,
From his vantage point in the tree,
He espies much activity
In a large garden nearby.
Gregarious blue tits feasting
On a fat ball, full of vitamins,
Hanging in the wind from its spike

On the stout stanchion supporting
The fat ball, a feeder cage
Full of peanuts is being attacked
By greenfinches, blue tits and one
Goldfinch, before they are scattered
By a domineering great tit
Who attacks the nuts with relish.

Bits of the choice morsels drop
Like manna from heaven
To waiting sparrows, chaffinches,
And one carefree white wagtail.
The squirrel leaps on the crosspiece
Causing untold panic, before
Nonchalantly eating in style.

David Wynne

THE JACK RUSSELL PUPPY

Maeve has called her Jo-Jo
But she really should be Go-Go
A ball of sheer energy
So fast she's a streak
Of white black and tan
And oh so sleek

Her head on one side
She looks into your face
Then you are grasped in a fond embrace
Your face is licked clean
And your ears are chewed
Why can't she sit still, and just be good?

She attacks the cat with verve and vim
He tries to escape
I'm so sorry for him
She clings to his fur, as he rushes around
The only escape -
Is high up off the ground.

After what seems an eternity
She lies down with a sigh
Cuddled up on your knee
How tiny and sweet she looks; and then,
Look out! Take cover! She's awake again!

Phyllis Henderson

BILL THE CAT

I love my cat
His name is Bill
He sits upon my window sill.
His face is black
His paws are white
And through the flap he goes at night.
Where he goes
I do not know
He even goes out in the snow.
Bill calls me when the morning breaks
Asking for his tuna flakes,
Then hops upon the window sill
I love my cat
His name is Bill

J Vessey

ODE TO MY SPOTTY DOG
(In memory of my beloved friend)

As I return to my house once more,
With the big quiet garden and old front door,
To the house in which you used to bound,
It's an empty house now, there is no sound.
I stand a moment, and breath the silent air,
Feel the lonely feel of nobody there.
Although it's been now almost a year,
I still feel the void of not having you here.
As I sit down with my cup of tea,
I'm so aware of there being just me.
When I have a meal, drop a pea on the floor,
There's no one to gobble it up anymore.
What do I do with the last crust of toast,
Or the crispy bits on the Sunday roast?
There are no covers now upon the chairs,
At last the carpets are free of hairs . . .
There's no longer a fuggy doggy smell,
And I realise I miss that as well.
I had you as a very small pup,
Tended and loved you as you grew up.
So, it was important to me I was there at your death,
To cradle you close as you took your last breath.
Your grave's in the garden and you still feel near,
Where other pets lie that were also so dear.
If you've ever had a dog that has died,
You will understand how inside I cried.
It's because of the good times it hurts such a lot,
I realise now what a great dog I'd got.
Maybe one day I'll have another good friend,
Depending on what life's fate will send.
I have so much love I could give you see,
And maybe there's a dog that will want to love me.

Kate Laity

THE CAT

The grass disperses not a sound is heard
As the wiry figure stalks the bird
Not a sound in anger or a move too quick
As the prey looks around she becomes still as a brick
Now in range for the mighty charge
The shadowy figure poised sleek yet large
Its move is made no time is lost
The unaware prey pays the cost
After a while the bird becomes a bore
So on to the best chair and a jolly good snore
Perhaps tomorrow a mouse or a rat
But there's one thing for sure you can't escape from the wiry cat.

Pete Simmons

WAITING FOR MOTHER

He sits upon the window sill,
staring down the road to see,
her coming up the steep hill.
Heaven knows how long she'll be.

Anxiety and worry
are now etched upon his face.
He wishes that she would hurry.
Frightened, alone, in this place.

Now here she comes into view.
She calls to him from the street.
This he takes to be his cue -
to the door and her to greet!

Up and down, in a bustle,
happy now that she is back.
His second name is Russell.
But we all call him Jack!

Douglas Bishop

JASPER, THE NEIGHBOUR'S DOG

Our friend approaches across the way
Chinking noted, it is teatime of day
Running askew, customary style
Craft, charisma, ego, guile,

Tongue out on one side balances the gait
Of a welcome visitor arriving late
Beaming hope and pleasure extreme
Wagging, laughing, glint and gleam,

Nostrils quivering, hastens within
Familiar route, checks his tin
Shining, empty, disillusion
Tail drops, dismay, mild confusion,

Jasper ventures a doleful glance
Enquiring, suggesting, a slip perchance
Chastised, humbled, we open a tin
Vigorously enjoyed, evil as sin.

Jack Pritchard

WHERE HAVE YOU BEEN?
(After an old Nursery Rhyme)

Blue Belle my Blue Belle
Where have you been?
I've been up to Windsor
To visit the Queen.

Blue Belle my Blue Belle
What did you there?
I left a pussy card
Under her chair.

Blue Belle my Blue Belle
What did it say?
It said 'Majesty, Dear Majesty
Have a good day.
With very best wishes
From Horatio and me
At the very start
Of your Golden Jubilee.'

Patricia Weitz

HORSEMAN

A nifty horse was Trigger his joy in life to run
and if at that you met a fence, he would jump it just for fun
he didn't need a bridle to keep him on the straight
or reigns to drive him faster for he was never too late
a trusted friend and partner he never took the stick
but if he didn't like you he would show you how to kick

He stood on hoof of Swedish steel stooped at heel
and there before the blacksmith kneel
the days have come and gone the season in its arc
now old Trigger's pensioned off he's lost his vital spark
a laying in the stable henceforth from where he grew
and sad to say it's possible he'll have to go for glue

John M Heddle

FAREWELL

Rest well, my friend;
Your wide brown eyes, eloquent as a sonnet,
Are closed for ever now in peaceful sleep.
The garden has lost an irreplaceable ornament,
Our lives a warmth that will be hard to find again.
Those walks will never seem the same
Without your pounding, excited feet
That scorched the lane or field or track.
The house is quiet, too quiet,
Without your reminding call
That urged us to open that door, or fill that bowl.
Thank you, my friend,
For all those years you were my friend.

Arthur W Gilliland

ITCHY

The past tense will never suit you, Itchy
wherever you are roaming now
I will always recognise your gait
so elegant, almost ethereal
it doesn't belong to our materialistic world
I know you are watching
our every gesture, our every step
be they lofty or innocent
perking your ears for our murmurs
our sighs, our bad temper
your splendid striped coat is that of eternal youth
you are the Egyptian goddess of yore
the modern diva of the digital era
playing each role
with an equally regal poise
putting our human arrogance
our pettiness to shame
yet, dear Itchy
it would be foolish to deny it
and you wince at any sign of hypocrisy
we will miss your girlish manners
your insistent complaints
whenever a visitor comes to your house
and he or she is served a biscuit
while your three plates
are brimming over with delicacies
you want to be reminded of your rank
and indeed, you were
and shall always remain
Itchy, the Empress of Cats

Albert Russo

RIVERSIDE

Emperor Dragonfly flying
Above nettles and reeds
Along the riverbank.
Summer heat and golden light,
Blue winged beauty
Beneath a deep blue sky.
The water green
Reflecting willows in leaf,
The dragonfly turns, pivots.
Hunting for prey amongst leaves,
Settling on its legs,
Fluttering low upriver.
Chasing insects in flight,
Delicate as a flower petal,
A duck could mistake
The deep blue robed
Hunter for a fluttering
Leaf but lunge with sharp beaks!

Janet E Smith

POPPY

Poppy was a ginger cat
I will always remember that
With my uncle Roy, Poppy did abide
She would never be one to hide
Poppy was very sweet
And always did keep neat
Her heart was warm
She did not like a storm
She got slower as she got older
Liking being beside the fire as it got colder
Poppy had her favourite chair
She always went to there

Sunil Hiranandani

RELEASE

Why can't pet cats live forever?
Good doctor vets be extra clever?
Feline grows the kitten fades
Amber eyes now serenade
Shimmering fur soft to behold
For our one they're seven old
A life span goes rushing by
No longer keen and bright of eye
Fur now feels like crumpled silk
As pink tongue slowly laps the milk
Must face facts the time has come
In skilful hands the pulse soon gone
Try to smile and walk away
From that hard table where you lay
Return to face an empty hearth
A sob that turns to trembling laugh
How long will this hurting stay?
Release love on a shivering stray

Winifred Smith

TOWN FOX

'Tis no 'Yo-ho-and away I go'
Just 'Woe-oh woe is me'
'For I am now a town fox
And pride 'tis history,' howls he,
'And pride 'tis history.'

Foxy went a-hunting as cruel North Wind did bite:
Slinking through dark shadows, that spurned electric's light.
Humbled was poor foxy, cruel fate did sadness bring,
Mem'ries now tasty voles, that scampered 'mid the ling.

Concrete was a-towering, where foxy used to play:
Speeding wheels killed mother: so foxy moved away:
Home's a filthy cellar, so dank: and oh so cold:
No sweet bed of grasses, for chicken thief so bold.

Vixen lay awaiting, with cubs that numbered five;
Foxy he was worried: How could they all survive?
Why was man the master of such devouring greed?
Would they see the future, as land they endless bleed.

Pictured swans, a-winging: and busy honeybees:
Daffodils of April, that danced with fragrant breeze:
River's dear companions, that swim her sparkling wine:
As from yard all littered, from swill-bins he did dine.

'Tis no 'Yo-ho and away I go:'
Just 'Woe-oh woe is me'
'For I am now a town fox:
And pride 'tis history,' howls he,
'And pride 'tis history.'

Violet M Corlett

AMBROSE THE CAT AND FRIENDS

What a nice day to meet some of my feline friends,
out from this kitchen window I will now descend,
they're outside in my overgrown garden somewhere,
first there will be Pinky the silver tabby there,
he is a very silly cat, he is nothing like me at all,
and rather fat, also unusually wide and very tall,
but why is he called 'Pinky' then? What a puzzle!
I hope the big dog next-door is wearing his muzzle,
this dog is named Rusty, and barks at us all the time,
and when he doesn't bark, he growls and also whines,
also Snowy the chinchilla, will be there without fail,
he will greet us with the usual swish of his tail,
I like Snowy, he is a very clever cat, I would say,
but not as clever as me, as I remind him every day,
Boris and Igor, both a Russian Blue, will be waiting,
they'll be watching us all, sternly concentrating,
the two of them are serious cats, I don't know why
Do they ever smile a lot I wonder? Or should I pry?
By the way, I'm a British Black Smoke Shorthair,
and I am Ambrose, a rather boring name to be fair,
everybody likes me, even Rusty, the noisy dog next-door,
even when I walk my dirty paws across the kitchen floor,
I see in the distance, that all my friends have come,
and that one of them is sniffing some other cat's bum,
another has made my garden smellier than a minute ago,
hopefully, towards me the wind will not surely blow,
there they all are, sitting, waiting for me to arrive,
here we are, first there were four, now we are five!

Christopher Higgins

BLACKIE

Blackie was our family cat
When I was very small.
She used to amble by my side
From the time I learnt to crawl.
She would sit there, purring at me
And give my face a lick.
Her eyes wide open, watching,
Her coat so smooth and thick.

Blackie was as black as soot
With eyes like liquid gold.
She had no malice in her,
An angel to behold.
Us children really loved her,
But we must have made her sore
With all the hugs and pulling,
But she'd come back for more.

She was always having kittens.
To us kids, it was just great.
Something else to play with,
But we never knew their fate.
They disappeared, one by one,
But Blackie did not mind
Because, a little later,
Another batch we'd find.

But her breeding days were over
When she had them in the bed.
My father took her to the vet,
Where certain parts were shed!
Blackie died at fifteen years,
And many tears we wept.
Of all the cats throughout the years
She was the best we'd kept.

Harry Gill

PRINCESS HONEY-BUN

Was there ever a little cocker spaniel so dear
always willing to show that you care
with the incline of your head
you understood what was said
even though you'd pretend not to hear?

Your eyes amber pools full of fun
always seeking for the mischief to be done
sizing up the world in a glance
never leaving anything to chance
in your effort to remain number one.

With your cute little furry panda feet
and your waggly bot that's so sweet
to your scruffy top-knot
with its kissable white spot
you managed to charm everyone you would meet.

Now I miss all our cuddles
all your messes and muddles
and those days when you wouldn't let up
you nicked food from our plates
and escaped out of gates
O our wonderful, crazy cocker pup.

D E Cornell

THE CONFUSED PUPPY

I sit there quite silent, I can't work it out.
One minute he's friendly, the next he does shout.
I try to keep him warm; I lie on his feet
And when he comes home, I always do greet.

I guard all his records, and music box thing.
I even join in, when he tries to sing.
I lie on his feet when he's in his chair,
I nuzzle up close to show him I care.

I eat all the scraps so there is no waste.
Even the curry, and I don't like the taste.
I try to be clean and run to the door.
But he never listens so I soil on the floor.

I sleep all the day so I'm active at night.
Stalking the shadows, I'm ready to fight.
If a noise I do hear I warn with a growl
And when he is snoring I join in and howl.

I give them my love I don't ask a reward
And things that I damage are just 'cause I'm bored.
I wish he'd not shout when I make a mess,
Like killing his slipper or Mummy's new dress.

But this time I've done it he really is mad,
The children are crying, 'Don't hurt him Dad.'
But the slipper I chewed must be worth quite a score.
'Cause it's snowing outside and I'm out the door.

Garry Knowles

SANDY

I found her wandering in the street
She was soon to make our lives complete
She wasn't a full Staffordshire Bull
But we love her as if her pedigree was full.

She followed me around on the day she was found
She wouldn't leave my side
I sent for the warden - she went to the pound
Her owners didn't want her around

Sandy's been with us two years or so
A nicer little dog no one could know
She barks quite loudly at a dog or a cat
Or at the postman when letters hit the mat

Sandy is truly a part of our life
She sits by the window and looks for the car
The welcome you get is second to none
The joy that she gives just goes on and on

She's a faithful hound she's always there
Sitting beside you sharing your chair
Staring adoringly into your eyes
Showing canine love and care.

Anthony J Gibson

BEARS

We all have many things to bear.
We have to bear up when things are bad.
Bear down and our lives are changed forever.
Bear the brunt when things go wrong.

Many have a bare-faced cheek,
And we all have to grin and bear it
When we have to go through something unpleasant.
Sometimes it becomes too much to bear.

We can be forced to bear when we are pressed,
And can we bear the strain when we are.
Bare naked is what we are when born,
When carrying a burden, can we bear the weight?

When like a bear with a sore head
Do we resort to bare knuckle aggression?
We sometimes bear our souls to a confidant,
All these bears shape our destiny.

Gladys Arthur

WELCOME ALL

What fun it is to love animals
For sure I just love them all,
They can be wild or tame,
Just take me amongst them
I'd love them all the same.

A ragged dog needs a good home
My cushion I give the cat,
Birds in cages all at song
When I sit down - my dog sits on my lap.

And not forgetting the wildlife
I break up bread for the gulls,
And 'Mr Robin' eats at my window box
These and many more, to me are pals.

Ducks and geese I love to feed
Old Foxy calls also to my door,
Some meat I save for him
Pets and wildlife I love for sure.

Horses should have a stable
In wintertime so cold,
A place to rest
I feel sorry for the lame and old.

So I'll give out all the love I can
While our good Lord lets me do,
And I pray, dear God
Let there be a heavenly home
For all of them too.

Marion Staddon

SAM THE SPANIEL

Those doleful eyes and floppy ears
Brought me endless bliss throughout the years
You were always there to be my friend
We saw it through to the very end.

Your frantic search for bone or ball
Beneath the earth by the garden wall
Kept me amused for hours and hours
Although you ruined all my flowers.

To lose you was such a pain to bear
As all our troubles we did share
I'll always love you until the day I die
Now you're in that bone yard up in the sky.

If there's a heaven for dogs I know you're there
Wagging your tail as I offer this prayer
Man's best friend you were to me
In every way there could possibly be.

Philip O'Leary

OUR RUSTY

He looked so forlorn tied up with a rope
Dejected and miserable - quite without hope.
No tail that wagged - no eyes that lit up
Though he was little more than a pup.

Someone took him off to an animal farm
So that he would come to no harm.
He stayed there a week but no owners were found
Though his particulars were passed around.

We then went to see him - my God, he was huge
This big German Shepherd at the animal refuge.
And needless to say we brought him home
And hope that he now will never more roam.

He lives for his walks now. We take him to parks
He plays with his friends but seldom barks.
Now he's properly fed, he's filled out his frame.
He's healthy and lively and loves a good game.

We've had him a year now and he's such a good boy.
He's bright and he's perky and he brings us much joy.
He's loving and giving and such a good pet.
We hope we've got years of loving him yet.

Jennie Rippon

WAITING

The war had lasted six long years,
And every night, he'd stayed
In stoic vigil, by the gate,
Hopeful and undismayed.

Dread bombs had fallen bringing death,
Shrapnel rained whining hate;
Yet still he waited patiently
Beside the garden gate.

One day, his master would return,
Warming, with firm caress,
The faithful hound greeting his lord
With boundless happiness.

Alas for canine loyalty -
His god, ambitious yet,
Spread out new roots in foreign soil . . .
Oh, *how* could he forget?

Beryl M Smith

CAT!

Independent is the cat,
Intelligent and worldly wise.
It never does the thing one asks,
Instead, it stares with hooded eyes!

Its gaze, all-knowing, ages old,
Reduces man to proper size.
Within a trice the cat is Queen,
The human race is hypnotised!

To undertake what cat decrees,
Albeit, food, or out, or play,
The strict demands must never be
Ignored, or scorned at, just obeyed.

When rules are firmly understood,
Cat may become a lifelong friend,
Desire to stay, to share your bed,
Your cupboards, drawers, it all depends!

June Cooper

FELINE FRIEND

You came when I was feeling low,
Because you had nowhere else to go.
A dirty bedraggled ball of fur,
Still you remembered how to purr.
A pat with a towel, a saucer of milk,
Your fur began to feel like silk.
Purring gently as you did from the start,
You wormed your way into my heart.
My world was feeling decidedly blue,
But that's all changed because of you.
You're here to stay my feline friend.
A happy note on which to end.

E Timmins

JINKY THE BUDGIE

As free as the wind, Jinky does roam
She lives in and loves her very own dome
As blue as the sea, how lucky can she be
Because she's a girl who's loved by you and me?
Jinky's all heart and has eyes like a dart
And she's a pet who's happy just to take part
At night she likes to climb onto her swing
And as she begins to nod, she gives her bells a little ring.

William Watt Jnr

ENTERPRISING BLACKBIRD

A blackbird was hopping around
tugging earthworms out of the ground,
but as twilight drew near,
he chirped, 'It is clear
what I need for the night
is a strong inner light,'
as he captured a glow-
worm to show
how he might 'watch and glow'!

Muriel E Critoph

LUCY

She sits upon my lap,
Gazes lovingly at me,
I see myself reflected in her eyes,
I wonder what she sees.

Does she feel my happiness when I'm glad?
Does she feel my sorrow when I'm sad?
Who can tell what she perceives
As she gazes lovingly at me?

I sense her deep devotion,
Her need to cuddle up,
She yawns and stretches, her paw touches my face
As if to say, 'Are you still awake?'

I look at her beauty,
Her feline green eyes,
I'm so glad I have her,
My beautiful cat.

M P Holmes

PUFFIN

My subject's that singular bird
Which some critics describe as absurd.
Your average puffin's
As plump as a muffin
With a nose occupying one third.

It's a rainbow-hued, colourful fellow,
Stripy-beaked, grey-blue, scarlet and yellow.
Splendid waterproof feathers
Foil the wettest of weathers
And its feet are like tangerine jello.

It produces a baritone note
Which it regurgitates from its throat.
Some intolerant folk
Say this sounds like the croak
Of a somewhat tone-deaf guillemot.

Just imagine how lonely it feels,
Out at sea, far beyond Galashiels,
With no books and no telly,
Always filling its belly
With mouthfuls and mouthfuls of eels.

Thus its flesh has a distinctive flavour
Which a few in the know like to savour.
Plucked and stewed, it's a dish,
Partly fowl, partly fish -
All you need is the puffin's cadaver.

So when next you are on the Bass Rock
And feel peckish, try boiling an auk
In a saucepan. For stuffin',
I recommend puffin -
It's a cross between kipper and cork.

Faith Bissett

DOLPHINS

The dolphins swim throughout the sea
and jump the ice-topped waves.
They glide beneath the water
to the underwater caves.

They swim around the seaweed
and glide about the wreck.
They swim down to the once sailed boat
and play upon the deck.

They swim throughout the blue lagoon
throughout the night and day.
Once more they swim beneath the sea
And leave the sunny bay.

Lyndsey Cubis

THE DOLPHINS

As a child I saw the dolphins
At play in Tampa Bay
They gambolled in the boat's white wake
And then they swam away

Then, off the bow,
Two grey fins sliced the blue-black sea
Two bodies arched above the waves
Wild, alive and free

Another three trailed astern
Diving, rising through the swell
There we watched in pleasured awe
Whilst the dolphins cast their spell

Around us played the dolphins
In their wondrous symmetry
Their charm and graceful beauty
Spoke of peace and harmony

Ray Ryan

AMPHIBIAN

When we met it was night
sleazy with rain,
polishing a dark world under lamp glow.
Cold, motionless light
slashed towards me from the house.

I didn't hear you speak,
just sensed concussion waves
rocking the air like bass drum vibes
buffeting and beating in my throat.

I caught your message in my pulse
and didn't fear
because it felt of wonder - yes, and love -
that we should meet in autumn in the dark,
your present time collapsing to my past.

I only feared when you picked me up,
painful alien warmth irradiating my nerve roots
when I wanted sleep.
You wondered at my hunched black skin,
the saurian nodules, goitred ogling eyes
and outreach with four tiny fingers to
the freedom of damp grasses, mouldering leaves.

And then you let me go back to my darkness,
damp of pond banks under stones,
and overtake your day
and you and all your kind into the night
when time shall stop.
I shall fill your unlamented space with my myriad progeny
as I have done before.

As I have done before.

John H Hope

IT'S A DOG'S LIFE

'Butter wouldn't melt,' me mom says
As she raps me once more on the nose
I've only been in the washing
And separated the socks from their toes

I love me mom and try to help,
With chores like washing and drying
I stick my head in the tumble drier
She knows I'm only trying

She gave me a shower the other night
I'd been in next door's pond
I'd clambered over the garden fence
Of this I'm rather fond

We play this little game you see
Mom calls me and I run
She calls me till I'm far away
I find this lots of fun

And as she puts her shoes on
And marches up the neighbour's path
I climb back over the garden fence
I find this such a laugh

When me dad is in the garden
And planting all his flowers
I go back out and dig them up
I like to fill his hours

I wouldn't change them for the world
I'm glad I chose these two
The best mom and dad a dog could want
Now where's that juicy shoe?

Tina Garrington

DOOR KNOCKER
(To Sophie)

She knew
Sophie dog who hated the vet
who had to be dragged in
lifted onto the table for examination
then if staying
must be carried into the inner sanctuary
only this time she walked
straight to the door
looking up for it to be opened
the door with healing hinges
the vet acknowledged that she knew first
only this healing
for the first time
in her fourteen years
was eternal.

Robert D Shooter

BILLY BUNTER

Unaware of the hunter,
In June's damp squib showers,
Sits fat Billy Bunter,
Unaware of the danger,
Which lurks in the flowers.
This boss cat's no stranger,
Will hide here for hours,
Awaiting the moment
To slay a plump chick,
Naan bread-stuffed-full Billy
Would just do the trick!
But though he's rotund,
This starling's got clout,
Flies off squawking *'Yarroo!*
You fellows watch out!
They call me the fat owl,
But I'm no cat's dinner.
I'd fly even faster,
Were I a shade thinner!'

Alan Swift

BESS

You came into my life like a breath of fresh air,
A bundle of fluff without a care.
You were trouble from the very start,
But I loved you with all my heart.
So full of mischief and full of fun,
I knew at once you were the one.
A free spirit without a care,
We were made to be a pair.
You have brought back childhood memories to me
Of a time when I was young and free.
And you have taught me, Bess, the meaning of life,
Just be yourself and forget the strife.
You are a one-year-old dog but oh so clever.
Thank you, Bess, I'll love you for ever.

Robert Beach

PUSSY DEAR

Oh Pussy dear, come play with me,
I am as lonely as can be,
I love your fur and big blue eyes,
I promise you a big surprise.

We will have a picnic on the lawn,
We'll spread a blanket on the grass,
And wave at everyone as they pass,
It will be such fun, you wait and see,
And we can sit under the apple tree.

I'll ask my mummy for some food,
A fish for you, a cake for me,
And maybe she will make us tea,
We will be as happy as can be,
Oh Pussy dear, please play with me.

Terri Brant

BERKELEY

He came to live here when he was a kitten,
He hid under my bed for two whole days,
And two days it took him to reach the kitchen:
So shy was he.

He went on the rooftop,
The train driver next door yelled:
'If that kitten comes on my roof . . . '
But Berkeley persisted, the train driver resisted:
We won the day.

When the train driver left he put down some poison -
Some poison for Berkeley, who had done him no harm.
'Epsom salts,' said the RSPCA -
I still don't know.

He's six years old now and still in a flat -
We've been trying to sell for such ages.
Always I've longed for a garden for him.
I hope it won't be too long.

For cats such as he should be happy and free -
Free to roam wherever they like.
Grass, trees, flowers and mice,
Soon all these will be his.

A Hankey

BEN

One day, it was on my birthday, my mum called me in for my tea.
I opened the door and there on the floor a pup was staring at me.
I'll never forget to this day - the thrill that I had in my heart.
I realise now I am older, the moment a friendship can start.

I cannot think of any friend who's been with me through thick and thin,
He's always pleased to see me no matter what mood I am in.
His eyes are as wide as the heart that's inside - he cheers me up
when I'm sad.
One thing I can say, from that very first day - he's the best friend
that I've ever had.

Tony Armitage

TANYA

With that sad look upon your face,
Those big brown eyes and golden hair.
Although you can't talk I know that you are there.
I am glad that you are beside me in my home.
That is why I don't feel alone.

When you give me your paw and lick my face,
It makes the world outside seem a better place.
So when I feel down I only have to look around.
I can see you wagging your tail and it makes me feel good.
I will love you to the end,
My faithful four-legged friend.

Sylvia Brown

FOREVER FRIENDS

My cat and I
Live side by side;
How fat
My cat
And I
Have tried
To be.

Nicola Barnes

REDEEMING TRAIT

When I was very, very small,
Playing with dolls and toys
I thought all pussy cats were girls
And puppy dogs were boys.
For pussy cats all liked to wash
And preen themselves all over,
While puppy dogs would roll in dirt,
Wet on the floor and slobber.
The little cats were ladylike
And ate with daintiness,
While little dogs all gulped their food
And made an awful mess.
The doggies were so clumsy,
Knocked little children down,
While pussies, like ballerinas,
Were light as feather down.
And puppies were like silly clowns,
And always made such noise,
While pussy cats were dignified
With quiet queenlike poise.
But as I grew, my prejudice
Against the dogs did change
In spite of all their grievous faults
And failings - the whole range,
For one day when I'd been scolded
And wept in deep disgrace,
A little doggie sympathised
With me, and licked my face.

V M Archer

CHARLES

Charles Foxall
A dog, a lovely boy is Charles
My friends, Kenton Foxall and Lisa Newey's dog
A lovely friendly dog, nice boy is Charles.
Loves to play and walk does Charles
Black and brown is Charles
Always barks at the hoover does Charles
Always excited when Kenton arrives home from work
Charles has been on many outings with his owners
Kenton Foxall, yes a good owner is Kenton.
Lisa Newey, a good owner is Lisa
Charles loves his owners
A lovely fabulous dog is Charles
I've looked after him on occasions
He was a friend of my late dog, Gino.
Charles doesn't mind cats
Kenton and Lisa have five cats
So Charles is used to cats
So Charles lives with them happily
No problems no trouble he likes them
They get along with no trouble
My friends Kenton and Lisa's dog Charles
Lovely boy is Charles
Nice boy is Charles
Yes Charles
Charles Foxall.

David J Hall

OUR DIFFERENT PETS

To one living alone, an animal can be more than a pet
Especially to someone who is trying hard to forget,
The pain of losing a loved one very dear,
Then a pet can be a constant source of cheer.

A dog makes a good companion and loyal friend,
One on whom you can rely and certainly depend,
Show him his lead and his tail wags overtime,
To deprive him of 'walkies' would be a crime.

A kitten is a furry bundle of playful fun,
Enjoying being cuddled by everyone,
Chasing the birds, then vanishing into trees,
To excited youngsters, a challenging tease.

The little canary, with its cage in the sun,
His sweet song sounds enchanting to everyone,
So different from the parrot with its harsh squawk.
Intermingled with words whilst trying to talk.

Children's small pets, mice, hamsters and rabbit
It's good for children to get into the habit,
Of feeding, grooming and being able to care
For pets, with whom their lives they will share.

And lastly the horse, who takes pride of place,
With his stately gait and natural grace
Ponies that help children overcome their disabilities,
How lovely to see them enjoying normal activities.

E K Jones

CINDY LOU (SO GLAD YOU CHEW)

My wife said 'How do you fancy
A brand new friend for you?
She's a beautiful Labrador puppy
By the name of Cindy Lou.'

I said, 'Do you know what Labradors do?
Do you know how they chew?'
She'll be my perfect get-out clause
For not having to buy any furniture new.

When she's not chewing bookcases
She's chewing the carpet bare
But she brings us so much happiness
She can chew from here to there.

Keith Large

ALL SPARE PARTS

They're over shot,
That pair of jaws,
And what
A motley set of paws.

Attached to legs
Too long to match
A body clothed
With scruffy thatch.

Those ears don't even
Make a pair.
Two ragged snippets
Hanging there.

But, through the eyes
That gaze at me,
Your doggy soul
Is plain to see.

Faithfulness
That never ceases,
Though built with
Ill assorted pieces.

Donald Harris

MEG

You warm my feet when they are cold.
You embrace my heart when it is bruised.
You demand I walk when I am weary.
You stalk my Hoover when it's in use!

You never shout when I am grumpy.
You comfort me in times of stress.
You keep me safe from delivering postmen.
You turn my home into such a mess!

You're always there when I need a friend.
Your devotion is beyond compare.
But please, dear Meggy, can I ask you,
Could you not shed so much hair!

Tree

CLEO'S DELIGHT

Cleo was our first Great Dane,
a bitch of beauty, hence her name.
Alas our 'Clee' was highly strung
and all she'd eat was fresh horse dung!
This performed a dual function,
Tasty morsel, perfumed unction.

We tried our best to make her eat,
boiled whole sheep's heads, a special treat.
Frozen tripe folks said she'd relish,
but the pong was awful hellish.
We opened every sort of tin,
but 'Clee' went down to bone and skin.

Friends said make her dinner piquant,
try any sauce you think she might want.
We tried them all including mustard,
but all that 'Clee' desired was custard.
Not as a main course, just a dipper
with lamb and beef, but mainly kipper.

This gourmet fare gave Cleo strength,
she grew in height and breadth and length.
Once more a beauty much acclaimed
a reputation quickly gained,
for a very peculiar appetite,
kippers and custard, Cleo's delight.

Jenny Sykes

BECKY (A MUCH LOVED DOG)

Don't cry for me, Mum.
I've loved you down the years
and wouldn't want the laughter
to turn to bitter tears.
Let your heart remember
the times of love we had.
The years we had together
can now outweigh the bad.
Close your eyes and see me still
I loved you then
and always will.

Gladys Mary Gayler

DOLLY

I have the sweetest little dog,
That I have ever met,
She's good natured, and contented,
And she makes the ideal pet.
She follows me, like a shadow,
Every move I make,
And she paws me every morning,
To make sure I am awake.
I only got her five days ago,
And she is five years old,
But I instantly fell in love with her,
Curly ears and coat of gold.
My wee darling's name is 'Dolly',
And she's a cocker spaniel bitch,
But she'll make my life more contented,
Than being famous or rich.

Jean Hendrie

THE BORDER COLLIE

The border collie, swift and sleek,
As he runs around his sheep.
With twists and turns as he runs,
To him it is a lot of fun.

His ears are tuned to each command,
As the shepherd alone he stands.
Through the ferns and the trees
Both collie and the sheep are free.

It is such a sight to see
Sheep controlled by one collie,
As the shepherd gives commands,
'Cum by,' or maybe 'Stand.'

The shepherd and one dog,
Through the rain, mist and fog.
But alas it's true I know –
One shepherd, one dog, proudly go.

Frank P Martin

WATER-LILY AND BUTTERFLY

A butterfly alights upon a lily pad,
waiting for a moonbeam, to dream of casting
dancing shadows of love. Zephyrus wings flirt
with Diana's lake, swaying among lotus flowers.
Attracted by the water lily, the butterfly hovers over it
ecstatically. She grows kaleidoscopic, turning into
a tiny nymph. She finds herself embraced by
an Adonis. Cupid hits them with a golden arrow,
and little by little, the truth awakens them.
You were my beloved in a previous life. That's why
you feel attracted by my leaf to rest on. We cherish
the memory of light, a cataract of past mysteries.
In this serenity of green dark, my fingers feel your magic,
and within your magic fluid, the birds exhale music.
Your eyes release joy into mine. I sense eternity.
You and I do not remember the past, for we are
a page torn out of an encyclopaedia of creation.
We have been a part of Adam's creation.
We'll meet again and again, for life is endless.
Overcome by a feeling of destiny, they hold each
other tenderly. A subtle breeze touches them.
Lotus bloom in the fields of water, vivid ballerinas
dance, and Cupids gallop and wave -
a glimmer in the air. How soon they turn again
into water-lily and butterfly and perform their last
waltz on the full-bloom lake, then dart about,
drifting in mystery - they disappear into the far
reaches of space. Mother Nature embraces
a withered water lily and a dead butterfly;
two lovers enter another world.

Najwa Salam Brax

SAM

My son came home with this ginger tom
He had been shut in a shed all day long
The poor wee thing had been eating wood
My boy said 'Please do what we could'
Its mouth was sore and its paws were raw
But the look in its eyes said he needed love more
A problem that we had to solve
Was with my boy's dad, as cats left him cold
The aviary he kept was his pride and joy
And to keep cats away was his daily chore
For two long weeks he wore a frown
But we knew we had finally won him around
I could not turn the cat away
So told my son that he could stay
We spent a fortune at the vet's
Anything going the cat would get
But gradually he did fit in
My son's dad took a liking to him
The years went by, my son left home
The cat stayed here no more to roam
By this time he was getting old
On our heartstrings he had a hold
When we saw he was fading fast
We knew this journey would be his last
With sinking hearts we seemed to know
Our Sam the cat was ready to go
To a resting place where pain would cease
After twelve long years, he will be at peace

Jean Dutfield

A VISIT

With keen delight I make my return to the park at Ewell Court -
offers me a chance to be close to a part of creation's wildlife
I take with me a well needed supply of bread -
nuts for the squirrels hidden in tall trees -
and as I share with them -
I am reminded there is more happiness in the giving –
than in the receiving – and so it is -
with wing creatures waiting there
for my visit in passing days of a year.

R P Scannell

SPUD

His mother just laid him down on the rug
Then licked herself clean and looking quite smug,
Turned up her face, looked me straight in the eye,
'There! You can have him! I'll see you! Bye bye.'

His eyes were tight shut, his paws clean and pink,
His nose was all 'snuffly' – well what could I think?
His ears were enormous compared with his head.
'Oh! Isn't he gorgeous?' someone else said.

'We'll get him a bottle, some food and a drink.
Just look at his eyes, see how they blink
He's ginger – a tom – not had one before.
Come on! Pick him up 'fore he wets on the floor.'

I whole heartedly loved him he was mine – mine alone.
We watched television, and spoke on the phone.
He covered me daily with long ginger hairs,
He purred on my lap and gave himself airs.

He'd sometimes get fleas or covered in lice.
I'd see them all moving – that's not very nice,
But we sat and I brushed 'til his coat was like silk,
Then gave him some salmon, chicken or milk.

He got very old and became very ill.
We went to the vet - I thought - for a pill.
'Oh dear' said the vet 'his chances are slim.
The way he is now is not nice for him.'

I wept and I cried for a week, maybe more.
I still see him lying down there on the floor.
I still hear his purr, I still miss him so.
It still makes me weep. Spud why did you go?

Audrey Chester

FEEDING THE BIRDS

The dressing up box has been raided:
a smudged-lipstick robin primps on the fence;
chaffinches parade in fancy costumes;
a single crow clatters along roof tiles
in Mummy's high heels.

Sparrows play hide and seek through the bushes
or dart out for a game of tag;
blackbirds prefer Grandmother's footsteps,
running and waiting, running and waiting,
scattered bread their goal.

Tits skip with clothesline,
waiting for their go on the swinging feeder,
while other birds bicker
over strewn-marble nuts.

School is out –
until unexpected movement
clears the playground.

Rowena M Love

OLD FAITHFUL

I do miss an old faithful friend of mine
Although it had short legs and no tail
Brown and white in its colour with blue eyes
Always let me know that it was about.

Alarming me to when the door bell rang
Or an odd cat nearby, with a bark,
Postman, has no fears at all delivering
For it was brought to me in my lap

Daily walks in the park so large
A bath in the pond chasing the ducks around
But not causing havoc, just playing with them
Till he got fed up of chasing them up and down

That's when they turned around and chased him off
With a last quack, as if to say see you again tomorrow
And a last bark, saying I will get you next time
Tired as he was, but lovable in every way

His age crept on as it always does
For it's now time to have its last dip
Before I say my very last goodbyes
For Shandy was the very best dog I had owned.

S J Davidson

THE BOOKSHOP CATS

Change is quite inevitable, or so it has been said,
The Bookshop now is up for sale. Sam's gone on ahead.
Delilah, Samson's sister, is left guarding on her own,
when the shop is sold and staff dispersed, she could be moving on.
Ten years they'd been in residence, The Bookshop Lytham Square,
Black Delilah was the home bird, ventures out were pretty rare.
Curled in her window basket, she'd sleep the days away,
oblivious to the people as they passed along the way.

Children pressing noses, squealing with delight,
the two cats curled up, fast asleep, a truly pleasing sight.
For Sam would often join her, in the window by the square,
a basket each they'd sleep the day, unfazed by public stare.
Pigeons round the Cenotaph were there for Samson's sport,
they saw him from a mile off but being the social sort.
They'd let him come up fairly close before they flew away,
Sam, philosophic'lly would feel. 'There is another day.'
The taxi drivers shouted, as he made those pigeons fly,
but with supreme indifference Sam would saunter on and by.

All the dogs with owners knew him. No matter what the breed,
one look from Sam and dogs were glad they were safely on a lead.
A tail cut short no one knew how and trips away in vans,
for Sam would sometimes sneak a ride, mess up delivery plans.
'Your cat's been half round Lancashire, we woke him up at Leigh,'
Sam yawned and stretched and sauntered in. 'Just in time for tea.'
So there he was all white and gold, the top cat, Lytham Square,
Everybody knew him as he strolled so debonair.
Sleeping on the still warm bonnet of a BM or a Merc
when the winter wind was blowing, he was not cut out for work.

But came that fateful August evening when Sam was out at play,
Hastings Place he met his end, it happened quick they say.
Now he's in another place where cars can't spoil his rhythm,
yet when those pigeons fly unspooked, could he be still in Lytham?
No matter what the future holds for the Bookshop Lytham Square,
years to come folk will remember, two sleepy characters there,
no matter what the shop purveys, paintings, handbags, hats,
They're going down in history, The Lytham Bookshop cats.

Derek B Hewertson

THE FERAL CAT

Her hidden depths of crystal jade
Slant and glint in sunlit glade
That feline stretch, that regal pose
Deludes us all, it is a doze.
Arched in spring and soft on claw
The feral cat leads a life all its own
And does not need our love or home.

Ruth Bell

PETS

My pets come from the wild plains of Africa
and my distance from them was a measured space
these pets of mine come from the banks of the Koriba Dam
where the lioness feeds after her kill
where also the zebra, formed so beautifully
and giraffes munch the trees so daintily
the red, red ochre soil they walk upon
the crocodile on the banks of the Zambezi
the chase of the buffalo with their babies at their side
hippos surfacing at the riverside
all these, my pets I saw in '93
none of the animals hurt a hair on my head.
The herds of elephants with their young came to drink
                              when the sun went down.

I'm home once more, in the cold and damp of the UK.
My own domestic cat sits near to me
and he washes and stretches like my feline friends in Africa.
The Koriba Dam is at my door
Africa, my senses feel and smell
Africa!
Africa, once more.

D Brook

POOR OLD DOG!

My poor old dog! With saddened eyes
And drooping ears, forlorn he lies.
His friendly tail he feebly thumps;
I think he's really in the dumps!

He hasn't been well at all today.
(I wonder what the vet will say?)
Perhaps he's eaten something bad.
But there, he's such a greedy lad!

When *I* am sad, he'll comfort me,
By laying his head upon my knee
And gazing up with soulful eyes
To gauge my mood, he bravely tries.

'I know, old chap, you want to talk -
I tell you what, we'll take a walk.'
His ears prick up, and taking heed,
He dashes off to fetch his lead.

He's always full of bark and bounce –
I throw a stick, he'll race and pounce,
And bring it back with prancing joy
And wagging tail, the clever boy!

But not just now, I think, old chap,
I see you'd rather take a nap.
So lie there quietly, whilst you may.
Tomorrow is another day!

A R Wilson

GOATS

When goats were made, and they were heaven sent,
God had poor mortals very much in mind,
And sought about him for a way to find
A source of clothing and of nourishment,
Then, that same hand that made the firmament
Took bone and whisker of a special kind
With horns and hooves and sinews all to bind,
And made – a mighty source of merriment!
Then said he, as the watching angels grinned,
To see the creature prance and pirouette,
'I make this for my children of the Earth,
For, though they've often failed and often sinned
I love them still, and I would give them yet
Another gift. This one will bring them mirth!'

Dorothy Steadman

THE CAT

Old Egypt sleeps within her eye,
A transcendental mystery,
And all the pageantry of Nile
Has moulded her benignant smile.

Under her somnolence is hid
The thought that raised the Pyramid.
The scion of a sacred race
Met Cleopatra face to face.

The cat was the familiar
Of Tutenkhamen, Potiphar –
Her immortality secure
Like theirs, upon a tablature.

Greeks and Romans came and went –
Comets in her firmament –
All like shadows passing by
Her inscrutability.

Audrey J Smith

EXPERT ADVICE

He came to cast an expert eye
over my untidy garden
studied with solemnity
the crazy paving

wanton, gloriously wild
clematis and honeysuckle
frayed lawn edges spilling
over stones and steps

bald patches in herbaceous borders
trodden pathways, hiding places
behind expensive plants.

'Petunia and lobelia at the front,'
he spoke his thoughts aloud,
'hydrangea there and prune this hebe
to a proper shape

stately delphinium would aptly fill that space
and there, replace that grass
and honeysuckle wilderness
with alpines in a structured rockery
some shapely stones
a flowing stream . . . '

Enthusiastic barking cut him short
flower pots flew in all directions
'Mayhem' circled round the shrubs
and rolled ecstatically in blue aubretia bed.

'On second thoughts,' he said,
'your garden
is just perfect for your pets.'

Oonagh Twomey

THE TALE OF THE FOX

Listen while I tell you the tale of the fox.
He's been hunted and hounded,
And had a few knocks.
He's been chased at full gallop
Pursued by the hounds,
In fear of his life,
Over fields he would bound.
On highways he's dazzled,
And loses his life,
That is not all the problems
The end to his strife.
For the sprawl is fast growing,
Populations expand,
Taking his food, and the territory land.
Now he roots in the offloads,
Of humans' remains,
In dustbins, in gardens,
And down country lanes.
So sad that a creature so beautiful to see,
Could face all these terrors,
In a wish to be free.
Will you spare just a moment,
To reflect on his plight?
As a part of creation,
Let us join in his fight.

Yvonne Sparkes

PETS WE HAD

First a black dog called Douglas
Way back in 1971/2
He was sold a year later
When he was too big for you

Two cats, Fuzzy and Marmalade
Caused mayhem when they became
Twenty-two cats and the RSPCA
Took twenty away from home

Two dogs, Benji and Toby
Went for walks with us
Toby got run over
Then Benji disappeared, what fuss

Neighbours' daughters in the 1990's
Gave us a cat to love
It disappeared two years later
Up to pussy heaven above.

H G Griffiths

OUR PUPPY

Tail a-wagging, throaty barks, hoping to be heard,
You stand there so expectantly hanging on our words.
Rolling on your back now, paws waving in the air,
You want to have your tummy rubbed by anyone who's there.

You scramble to your feet again, run quickly to the door,
Sit upon your back legs now as you have done before.
You beg for a lump of sugar, we place it on your nose,
You toss it up and catch it, then down your throat it goes.

Now playing with your rubber ball
As you've done since first we bought it,
Then round and round you chase your tail
But what would you do if you caught it?

Looking for your lead now you hanker for a walk,
You make it seem so obvious - if only you could talk!
Our frisky little puppy full of playfulness and fun,
Keeps everybody busy - his demands are never done.

Pauline Anderson

IT'S NOT MUCH FUN BEING A CAMEL

We're known as ships of the desert,
A colourful, descriptive phrase;
It really means beast of burden,
And it's not a paean of praise.

It's not much fun being a camel,
They make rotten jokes about me;
What do they call one with three humps?
It has to be known as Humphrey.

People don't know they're so hurtful,
For even we camels have pride;
But some of their pointed comments
Get through my leathery hide.

We camels started in Asia,
Llama's a relation of mine;
As is the well known alpaca,
Which suits everybody just fine.

Then cigarette advertising,
Brings us royalties, every year;
I've no idea what they're made of,
And hope that it's not what I fear.

It's not much fun being a camel,
We've no pension that's index-linked;
Walking the Nile, the same silly smile,
Bearing up until we're extinct.

James Kimber

CHESTER

Come on Chester, let's go out!
It's walking time again
Let's get your lead and rubber bone
And both go down that lane
Whatever you do, don't 'cock that leg'
Or 'whoops' where folk may tread
It's quite a common problem
With you being so well fed
We'll have a chase and play around
And then a doggie chat
'Sit!' and 'Stay!' then 'Come on boy!'
And then a friendly pat
You are a really special chap
A loyal, loving friend
You wag that tail and guard the home
And a warning message send
You keep an eye on Ben and George
'Twas they that christened you
You'd just been born when they'd been off
To visit Chester Zoo
It's often said, you're man's best friend
Of course, we know that's true
But it's for sure, we are enriched
By simply being with you!

Frank Dean

A LAWN - TO BE OR NOT TO BE!

At times I'm envious of the smooth greensward,
Those pristine lawns that other people have:
But then I think, 'How boring!'

My lawn is more like some rough field
Attracting so much wildlife.
The busy squirrels, furry, grey,
With nimble fingers dig their holes
To hide the nuts that I provide,
Then on a cold and wintry day,
Like miners seeking gold they dig
To find their hidden store.
A myriad of birds with pointed beaks
Tweak up the grass and bits of moss
To line their nests as spring comes round
Or wrestle with the juicy worms
That live just underground.
The tawny fox with padding feet,
Following the same known route
Wears down the grass and forms a path
That I can clearly see.
Small insects scuttle through the blades,
I hear a cricket sing,
And large-eyed frog, well camouflaged,
Flicks lightning tongue for food.
Even my dog has no respect
But leaves brown dying patches.

Both wild and tame the creatures come
To traverse once smooth turf,
And though I sigh with envy still
When passing other gardens,
Yet I delight that I play host
To creatures great and small.

Roma Davies

THE KIPPER

The kipper is a versatile fish
You can serve it for breakfast
Or your main evening dish
It's very tasty alongside afternoon tea
With your old friend the kipper you're never at sea

    The kipper is a traditional fish
    Eaten by Churchill
    It was his dying wish
    To have a large kipper for his evening meal
    Enriched with some mustard and a cutlet of veal

        The kipper is an intelligent fish
        If you heed its advice
        Then in time you'll grow rich
        It knows all about money, emeralds and gold
        Have you ever seen a kipper-run company fold?

            The kipper is an athletic fish
            It can swim in marathons
            Without getting a stitch
            In gymnastic prowess it's the king of the sea
            All the young mermaids cry, 'It's a kipper for me!'

                The kipper's majestic
                    Let the kipper swim free
                        Though I hope that my eulogy doesn't sound twee
                        May its song be eternal
                        Pray the species stays strong
                        For with our ally the kipper
                        You can never ever
                        Well very rarely ever
                        Go wrong!

Stuart Delvin

WATCHING THE BIRDIES

My cat always watches when the birds are being fed,
She eyes them all with frozen stare when they swoop down for
the bread.
Occasionally she rushes out of her hiding place,
The poor alarmed birds all fly off back to base.
I know she'll never catch one, not because she's too slow,
Why can't she catch them? I'm sure she wants to know.
I know the reason and I'm not ashamed to tell,
That I've fixed up her collar with a jingle bell.

Anne Cooper

OUR LOVEABLE PUSSIES

Tia, Tabby, Teddy and Timothy,
Tia-Maria, Tammy, Thomas and Topsy
Much enjoyed one another's company
Singing together a song in harmony.
Passers-by would stop and throng,
Listening to their quite original song.
Filled with astonishment and admiration
They could hold with them a conversation.
Living now in a heavenly sphere above
Our pussies fill it with song and love.

M MacDonald-Murray

QUEEN OF THE LAKE

The swan she glides across the lake,
The water ripples in her wake,
Feathers upon her back so straight,
She looks around to find her mate,
This graceful swan she gently preens,
Of all the birds she is the queen,
Majestic head and snow-white down,
Without a doubt she wears the crown,
Her cygnets all around her crowd,
She moves among them, very proud,
These ugly ducklings will become,
Into wondrous swans, second to none.

W Curran

REQUIEM FOR AN AVENUE CAT

Far, far away, but closer, day by day,
How I miss your sleek black body
Surreptitious, in a hurry, painfully shy, slipping by
A canny wariness to your adventures on the sly.

At first, when I saw you, I thought 'Oh no!'
It's our beloved black cat 'Slinky' going where he shouldn't go.
But on reaching Lamorna Reach, our house, I was pleased to see
That our baby was safe, with you, thence with me.

I never knew your name, beloved feline friend,
A cat of Cliffe Avenue, Westbrook, proved your end.
Nine am'ish on the morning of Friday 11th January, 2002AD
I stopped, awaiting my bus into Margate you see.

There you lay, still on your side, mute and gone
Laid on the opposite pavement, left all alone
I prayed that God in His mercy and through the love of Christ,
Would hold you now in heavenly arms in climes, angelic bright.

A little while later, a neighbour appeared from her house on the corner
I said 'How sad' - she told me the lady motorist
Had knocked on her door, distraught, a little before -
She was anxious to locate his owner, to put their minds at rest.

A beloved pet gone, killed on the traffic-fast highway of
                              Westbrook Avenue
Name unknown, owners unknown, lost from our Isle of Thanet venue
Rest in peace, dear little furred friend,
I know that God Almighty lets you live forever and have no end.
                                                    Amen

Joy Sheridan

THE CAT

Just see the cat sat on your stuff,
He really doesn't care enough.
He doesn't care if you are stressed,
He wouldn't care if you were blessed.
If he gets 'treats' when he demands,
Then 'truly' life is in cats' hands.

H M Buckley

SO ANIMAL MAGIC

Just be cool,
I am just amazing
playing the fool,
But who did that stool?
It wasn't me
Just playing the fool
So animal magic
Be cool
And play your act at Blackpool.

Lynda Firth

AN EARLY FOX

Waiting to catch, an early bus.
One sees, in the dark and gloom.
Glimpse of the white tip,
Of a fox's furry brush.
In amazement, watch in hush.
See the gleam of green from hunting,
Nocturnal eyes.
Opposite the bus stop, gleaming bright.
One spies an urban fox.
Marking its bounds.
Alert to every sound.
He takes flight.
At switching on of house lights.
Sounds of workers getting ready for work.
Sleepy-eyed, not yet fully alert.
A blink of an eye, he's gone,
Like Will-O'-the-Wisp.
Weird how he disappeared into an early mist,
That covers a maze of alleyways.
Gardens, in and out ways.
Spooky the way he slipped away home.
A deep burrow beneath, someone's lawn.
Sleep till night, go hunting till dawn.

B Clarke

FROG HUNTER'S DAY

At Chippy's quarry, one summer's day,
The young frog hunter, he did play.
He laid and watched them spring all around,
He found his music, in their croaking sound.

Time has no concept, to a child having fun,
But it has to a mother, who's missing a son.
Above the water, on a branch he does perch,
As his mother begins her two-hour search.

She spots her son across the lake,
She shouts in fury, for the branch might break.
Wellies full of water, he runs to his mum,
Why are you here, what have I done?

Frog-marched home that visit the last,
So many summers, have now since passed.
But when tadpoles' tails, have gone away,
He fondly remembers, frog hunter's day.

Geoffrey Woodhead

FLUFFY IS MY DARLING

Fluffy is my darling,
        I really love him so,
his companionship a heaven-sent blessing,
        with a coat as white as snow.

His eyes are little diamonds,
        like the stars amidst the sky,
he is my guardian angel
        although he cannot fly.

He sits upon the window sill,
        watching for his little friend,
another fluffy white puss
        who lives around the bend.

The positions he sleeps in are hilarious,
        with legs wide apart and all,
sometimes dangling from the chair,
        yet he never seems to fall.

Fluffy is my darling,
        I'm glad that cats were made,
so we can still have companionship,
        when to rest - our friends are laid.

Steve Kettlewell

SILVERBACK

I'm a gorilla, proud and strong,
I live in the mountains and do no wrong.
I hide in the forest, away from man,
Please leave me alone and forget where I am.
Don't violate my home with your sickness and guns,
I will die soon enough when the time comes.
I would rather die now than grow old in a zoo,
I want to go my way, not be murdered by you.
Why struggle through jungle thick and hot,
Just to cut off my hands for your cigar butts?
If you must come near me, point camera not gun,
I don't know the difference and will not run.
If you must see my like, then go to the zoo
And gaze at my brother in his plight.
Gaze in awe at his magnificent size,
But notice the moisture in his eyes.
He's a silverback too, twice your size and five times as strong,
Please, please, leave us alone, we've done no wrong.

J Stenning

No Luck

A strange moggy entered the garden
    an aggressive look on his face
Stalking this way and that
    as if he owned the place

Studying each little bird
    deciding to take his chance
Chattering aloud, away they all flew
    wryly he looked askance.

Sniffing around the borders
    something aroused his suspicion
Pouncing on a terrified mouse
    had he accomplished his mission?

Being a big important cat
    he tossed his prey in the air
Tantalising the poor little beast
    'Miaow'! Run away if you dare

Looking to the window for admiration
    averting his eyes from the mouse
Too late he spied his prey
    scurrying towards the house

His attention-seeking allowed
    an escape into a hole by the drain
Most surprised and annoyed
    he searched and waited in vain

Slyly he skulked away
    losing really hurt his pride
His visit had gained him nothing
    not a tiny morsel inside.

Greta Craigie

TOAST AND MARMITE

(Dedicated to Marmite the guinea pig)

Marmite we know you've left our house,
Along with your friends, and our cuddly white mouse.
But now you're in a haven, with pals large and small,
In a place of wonder, with angels you can call.

With your mottled brown coat to keep out the cold,
The antics you showed us, were pure natural gold.
Memories held, of your passion for toast,
And digestive biscuits, (eaten by most).

Your squealing at mealtimes, when we walked past your hutch,
With lettuce piled high, it all seemed too much.
But eating was one of your pleasures in life,
It simply came first, in this world and its wife.

Although we can't see you, we know you're not gone,
You're still around us, while memories live on.
We'll miss your music, when mealtime was near,
For now you can slumber, with nothing to fear.

Janice Thorogood

ARCTIC DAYS ON A ROLL

The seals look up with obsidian eyes
As black as night skies
They swim and fish
Splash and swish
Through ice floes so rich
With hardly a hitch
In life that's so varied
Sea and sky married
To watch the seals swim so fast
To catch their breakfast
And avoid polar bears
To hide from solar flares
Seals and snow colours so pure
From white to purest azure.

Tim Sharman

ANIMAL MAGIC

I've loved animals
All of my life
I despise people
Who hurt them
They're not worth my 'hate'
For the animals
I've always tried to help them
Sometimes I'm too late

I have eight dogs
Seven cats too
All abandoned
All alone
Nowhere to go
They came to see me
Now they live together
With all the love
I can give
Their eyes no longer pleading
'Please help me somebody
For me to live'

I keep wishing
I could win the lottery
To help animals more
So the door
Could always be open
For the animals I adore.

Trisha Moreton

TO HAVE AND TO HOLD

My dearest friend came close to me when I was sitting all alone.
I shifted up to give him room, and we sat quietly in our home.
He sighed and drew much closer, I felt his breath upon my cheek,
Then he touched me very gently and I felt my knees go weak.
I placed a hand upon his shoulder, drew him closer still,
This love I feel is a rarity as I bend him to my will.
Ask 'Do I love him?' 'Deed I do, my lovely faithful friend,
In all the woes I've struggled thru he has seen me to the end.
When I declare my love for him 'tis excessive I am told,
That I ignore because I have a cat to have and to hold . . . indeed!

Rosie Hues

KITTEN

Contentment is a ball of fluff
Looking like a powder puff.
Two eyes stare in astonishment
And you know the fluff is pleasure bent.

Crash, bang, wallop, thump
Every sound makes you jump.
A trail of havoc marks its wake
You wonder just what next will break.

This used to be your domain
Now things will never be the same.
You sigh, you moan, you wonder why
And watch a ball of fluff streak by.

No crash, no bang, no hurried scurry
Now is the time you start to worry.
You look, you call, you plead, you cry
In the end you breathe a sigh.

There amongst the scattered plants
Completely out of puff and pant,
Is the reason you're completely smitten
A ball of softly sleeping kitten.

M A Honeyman

The Coal Fire's Glare

What dreams do you have lying there
So sleepy in the coal fire's glare?

In daylight bright I've watched you run
Across the fields 'neath blazing sun -
Down the paths and through the corn
Seeking - what? - on a summer's morn.
Nose to ground when scent was strong
You've hunted, gaily, carefree, long.
Now resting, coat as black as night,
So sleepy in the fire's light.
I wonder, do you long to be
Out in the country running free?

Or, as you tremble in your sleep,
Is it to be by rivers deep
Where, splashing through the reeds and muck
You might flush out a brace of duck?
Or would you be on hills of shale
Where eagerly you've chased the quail
And where you've pounced on rabbits fat
And careless in their habitat?
Are these the scenes you long to know
When basking in the fire's glow?

Yet, as you lie there, lithe and dark,
Perhaps you'd rather prance the park
And madly romp among the leaves
That, fallen, lie beneath the trees.
Or do your dreams turn to the strand
Where you may trot along the sand
And, barking, charge in to the race,
Retrieving sticks with easy grace
Before, once more, you stretch out there
So sleepy in the coal fire's glare?

Brian Beveridge